Yellow Umbrella Books are published by Capstone Press
151 Good Counsel Drive, P.O. Box 669, Mankato, Minnesota 56002
www.capstonepress.com

Library of Congress Cataloging-in-Publication Data
VanVoorst, Jennifer, 1972–
    Who builds? / by Jennifer VanVoorst.
    p. cm.
    Summary: Simple text and photographs compare some of the structures that
people build to those built by animals.
    ISBN 0-7368-2924-5 (hardcover)—ISBN 0-7368-2883-4 (softcover)
    1. Animals—Habitations—Juvenile literature. 2. Building—Juvenile literature.
[1. Animals—Habitations. 2. Building.] I. Title.
QL756.V36 2004
591.56'4—dc21   2003007739

Editorial Credits
Editorial Director: Mary Lindeen
Editor: Jennifer VanVoorst
Photo Researcher: Deirdre Barton, Wanda Winch
Developer: Raindrop Publishing

Photo Credits
Cover: Royalty-Free/Corbis; Title Page: DigitalVision; Page 2: Bruce Ando/Image Ideas,
Inc.; Page 3: DigitalVision; Page 4: Tomi/PhotoLink/PhotoDisc; Page 5: EyeWire; Page
6: Royalty-Free/Corbis; Page 7: Cliff Beittel; Page 8: PhotoLink/PhotoDisc; Page 9:
Hans Reinhard/Bruce Coleman, Inc.; Page 10: Jeremy Woodhouse/PhotoDisc; Page 11:
Ed Wargin/Corbis; Page 12: Mark N. Boulton/Bruce Coleman, Inc.; Page 13: Jen and
Des Bartlett/Bruce Coleman, Inc.; Page 14: David Toase/PhotoDisc; Page 15: Peter
Ward/Bruce Coleman, Inc.; Page 16: EyeWire

1 2 3 4 5 6 09 08 07 06 05 04

Who Builds?

by Jennifer VanVoorst

Consultant: Robyn Barbiers, DVM, General Curator,
Lincoln Park Zoo, Chicago, Illinois

Yellow Umbrella Books

an imprint of Capstone Press
Mankato, Minnesota

People build things to help them live.

Animals build things, too.

People build houses.

Animals build houses, too!
Foxes dig dens.

People build apartments.

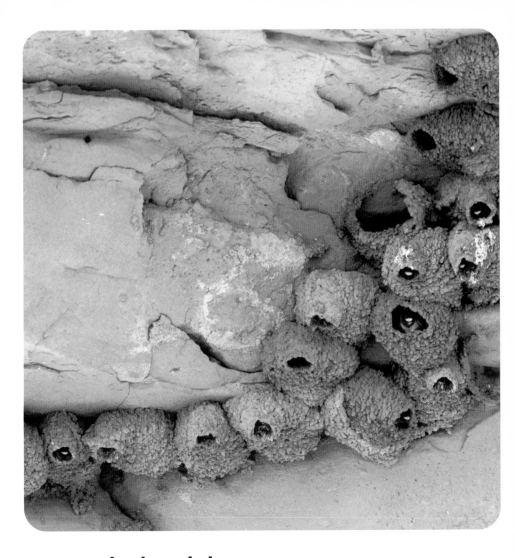

Birds build apartments, too!
These birds build their nests
close together.

People build tunnels.

Moles build tunnels, too!
Moles use their claws to dig.

People build bridges.

Spiders build bridges, too!
This spider web is a bridge
between blades of grass.

People build dams.

Beavers build dams, too!
Beavers build with mud and sticks.

People build towers.

Termites build towers, too!
This tower is as tall as a tree!

What do you build?

Words to Know/Index

Word Count: 97
Early-Intervention Level: 9